HISTORY OF THE CUP

THE ROAD TO THE
WORLD'S MOST POPULAR
CUP:

HISTORY OF THE CUP

MAKING THE FINAL 32

TEAM USA

TOP TEAMS

WORLD STARS

HISTORY OF THE CUP

Andrew Luke

MASON CREST

MASON CREST

450 Parkway Drive, Suite D | Broomall, Pennsylvania 19008
(866) MCP-BOOK (toll-free)

Andrew Luke

First printing
9 8 7 6 5 4 3 2 1

ISBN (hardback) 978-1-4222-3953-7
ISBN (series) 978-1-4222-3949-0
ISBN (ebook) 978-1-4222-7831-4

Cataloging-in-Publication Data on file
with the Library of Congress

QR CODES AND LINKS TO THIRD-PARTY CONTENT

CONTENTS

KEY ICONS TO LOOK FOR:

 Words to Understand: These words with their easy-to-understand definitions will increase the reader's understanding of the text while building vocabulary skills.

 Sidebars: This boxed material within the main text allows readers to build knowledge, gain insights, explore possibilities, and broaden their perspectives by weaving together additional information to provide realistic and holistic perspectives.

 Educational videos: Readers can view videos by scanning our QR codes, providing them with additional educational content to supplement the text. Examples include news coverage, moments in history, speeches, iconic sports moments, and much more!

 Text-Dependent Questions: These questions send the reader back to the text for more careful attention to the evidence presented there.

 Research Projects: Readers are pointed toward areas of further inquiry connected to each chapter. Suggestions are provided for projects that encourage deeper research and analysis.

 Series Glossary of Key Terms: This back-of-the book glossary contains terminology used throughout this series. Words found here increase the reader's ability to read and comprehend higher-level books and articles in this field.

Aggregate: combined score of matches between two teams in a two-match (with each often referred to as "legs") format, typically with each team playing one home match.

Away goals rule: tie-breaker applied in some competitions with two-legged matches. In cases where the aggregate score is tied, the team that has scored more goals away from home is deemed the winner.

Cap: each appearance by a player for his national team is referred to as a cap, a reference to an old English tradition where players would all receive actual caps.

Challenge: common term for a tackle—the method of a player winning the ball from an opponent—executed when either running at, beside, or sliding at the opponent.

Clean sheet: referencing no marks being made on the score sheet, when a goalkeeper or team does not concede a single goal during a match; a shutout.

Derby: match between two, usually local, rivals; e.g., Chelsea and Arsenal, both of which play in London.

Dummy: skill move performed by a player receiving a pass from a teammate; the player receiving the ball will intentionally allow the ball to run by them to a teammate close by without touching it, momentarily confusing the opponent as to who is playing the ball.

Equalizer: goal that makes the score even or tied.

First touch: refers to the initial play on a ball received by a player.

Football: a widely used name for soccer. Can also refer to the ball.

Group of death: group in a cup competition that is unusually competitive because the number of strong teams in the group is greater than the number of qualifying places available for the next phase of the tournament.

Kit: soccer-specific clothing worn by players, consisting at the minimum of a shirt, shorts, socks, specialized footwear, and (for goalkeepers) specialized gloves.

Loan: when a player temporarily plays for a club other than the one they are currently contracted to. Such a loan may last from a few weeks to one or more seasons.

Marking: defensive strategy that is either executed man-to-man or by zone, where each player is responsible for a specific area on the pitch.

Match: another word for game.

One touch: style of play in which the ball is passed around quickly using just one touch.

One-two: skill move in which Player One passes the ball to Player Two and runs past the opponent, whereupon they immediately receive the ball back from Player Two in one movement. Also known as a *give-and-go*.

Pitch: playing surface for a game of soccer; usually a specially prepared grass field. Referred to in the Laws of the Game as the field of play.

Set piece: dead ball routine that the attacking team has specifically practiced, such as a free kick taken close to the opposing goal, or a corner kick.

Through-ball: pass from the attacking team that goes straight through the opposition's defense to a teammate who runs to the ball.

Touch line: markings along the side of the pitch, indicating the boundaries of the playing area. Throw-ins are taken from behind this line.

Youth system (academy): young players are contracted to the club and trained to a high standard with the hope that some will develop into professional players. Some clubs provide academic as well as soccer education.

INTRODUCTION

How did the biggest sporting event in the world come to be so big over the past 88 years? First, let it be clear that we are referring to the FIFA World Cup here (FIFA is short for Fédération Internationale de Football Association). By every measure that matters, this global soccer tournament that takes place every four years is bigger than the Olympics, and far bigger than the Super Bowl. In America, the Super Bowl is still king, but when you consider its popularity across the whole planet, the Super Bowl is way down the list of top sporting spectacles, and is eclipsed by several soccer events, chief among them the World Cup.

The World Cup is not the best soccer competition in the world. That distinction probably belongs to the UEFA Champions League. The Champions League takes place every year in Europe (UEFA stands for Union of European Football Associations) and is a competition between the top-performing soccer clubs in Europe's best leagues. It plays out over a 10-month period, from July to the final match in May. The Champions League final regularly draws more than 350 million viewers— or about double what the Super Bowl typically draws—worldwide.

As almost all of the best players in the world play in European leagues, the Champions League is regarded as a best-on-best competition. The assembled talent on the top European club teams is considered to be better than that on top international teams—even on the best teams like Germany and Brazil.

The World Cup, however, is on a different level. About 190 million people watch each match, making every one of the matches like a Super Bowl. For the final, about one billion people tune in to watch, or nearly three times the Champions League audience.

What the World Cup brings that is so captivating, that goes beyond the quality of the teams and the skill of the players and the passion for the sport, is that element of nationalism. Over the decades since 1930, the competition has catered to the national pride that participating nations feel, as well as to the pride all other nations aspire to feel one day when their team might qualify.

In an increasingly global culture, soccer is a common thread, and hopeful Japanese viewers can relate to the expectant fervor of a Brazilian fan, as well as the pride of Bosnians watching their team compete for the first time. The World Cup is truly the world's cup.

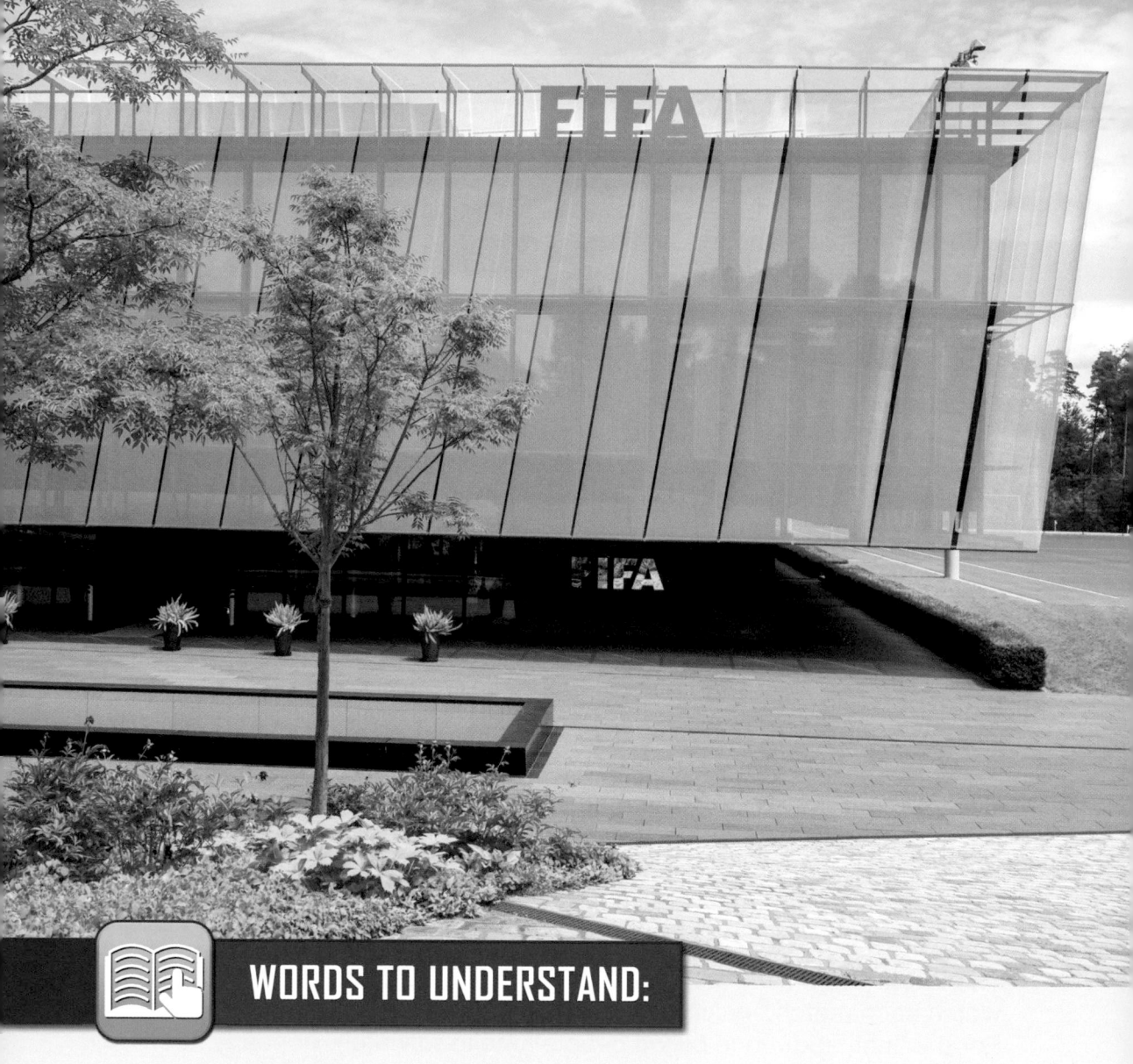

WORDS TO UNDERSTAND:

boycott: to engage in a concerted refusal to have dealings with a person, a company, an organization, etc., usually to express disapproval or to force acceptance of certain conditions

contention: a state or condition marked by a lack of agreement or harmony

revert: to come or go back (as to a former condition, period, or subject)

CHAPTER 1

THE BEGINNINGS (1930–38)

In the early part of the twentieth century, soccer was still trying to find its way as a sport that people could get behind. Soccer's international governing body, FIFA, had been founded in 1904 with just seven countries: Belgium, Denmark, France, the Netherlands, Spain, Sweden, and Switzerland. The real influence behind attempts to internationalize soccer at the time was the Football Association (most of the world calls the sport *football*, not soccer).

The Football Association (FA) is based in England, and was founded in London in 1863. The FA came up with a common set of rules to lend some consistency to the sport. Forty years later, the FA was still the most prominent governing body. For the Olympic Games, for example, it was the FA that organized the Olympic soccer tournament in both 1908 and 1912. These were the first true tournaments at the Olympics and the first instances of national rather than club teams representing the participating nations.

Jules Rimet, honored by this Paris street in his name in his home country of France, was elected president of FIFA in 1921 and staged the first World Cup in 1930

FIFA added five members between 1904 and 1913, including the United States, but the organization struggled to survive during World War I. The FA again organized the first post-WWI Olympic tournament in 1920. But in 1921, Frenchman Jules Rimet was elected FIFA president, and things began to change for the association. FIFA took over the staging of the Olympic tournament in 1924, and did so again in 1928.

In 1928, Olympic organizers decided not to include soccer as an event at the following Olympic Games. The reason for this was that the 1932 Games were slated for Los Angeles and organizers feared that American audiences would not show up for the matches due to the low popularity of the sport in America. At this point, Rimet decided that this was the perfect opportunity for FIFA to stage its own championship every four years, one where professional players were welcome to play, unlike at the Olympics. Allowing professionals to play had long been a point of **contention** between FIFA and the International Olympic Committee.

1930 World Cup

Rimet chose Uruguay as the site of the very first FIFA World Cup, and scheduled the tournament for 1930. Uruguay had won the previous two Olympic soccer gold medals. European countries were not happy with the selection of a South American location, and all said they would skip the event. Eventually, Rimet was able to convince France, Belgium,

Still in use today, the Estadio Centenario in Montevideo, Uruguay, was the site of the very first World Cup final match in 1930

Romania, and the former Yugoslavia to participate, making 13 teams in total.

To the surprise of no one, the powerful Uruguayans went undefeated through four matches. Playing in front of their passionate home fans, they gave up just three goals in all, while scoring 15 themselves.

The final matched Uruguay against Argentina, and more than 90,000 fans jammed Estadio Centenario in the capital, Montevideo. The La Plata River separates the city from Argentina, and Argentines crossed the river by the thousands to support their team, led by the tournament's top scorer Guillermo Stábile. Spectators were treated to an entertaining match, as Argentina took a 2–1 lead into halftime. The quality of the Uruguay side was too much, however, and goals 11 minutes apart by Pedro Cea and Santos Iriarte put Uruguay ahead to stay. The match ended 4–2, and the following day was declared a national holiday.

1934 World Cup

Rimet was under the heavy expectation that the next World Cup would be held in Europe, and Italy eventually won out over Sweden to be the host in 1934. Following the success of the first event, 36 countries petitioned to be included, so qualification matches were held to select 16 teams. The United States was one of six teams to qualify that had played in the 1930 event as well.

One significant change in 1934 was that the tournament used a knockout format only; meaning that there was no group stage this time around. As a result, the four teams that had traveled the farthest to participate—Brazil, Argentina, USA, and Egypt—were all eliminated after playing just a single match. The eight teams that won and advanced past the first round were all European.

The second, or quarterfinal, round featured some tight matches and rough play. All four matches were decided by a single goal. The host Italians, for example, tangled with Spain in a match where midfielder Mario Pizziolo had his leg broken in a vicious tackle. The match was tied at 1–1 after regulation and 30 minutes of extra time had been played. There was no penalty kick shootout in those days. Rather, the rules called for the match to be replayed the following day. In the second match, the rough play continued, this time resulting in three Spanish players suffering match-ending injuries. Italy won 1–0 to advance to the semifinals.

Austria's Wunderteam were the favorites to win the 1934 World Cup, but lost in the semifinals to host, and eventual champions, Italy

Italy's semifinal opponent was Austria. The Austrians were known as the Wunderteam (meaning Wonder Team) and were the favorites to win the World Cup. Over a 20-month span ending in 1932, the Austrians had won 14 matches in a row. However, in another tightly contested match, and in poor weather conditions, Italy again won 1–0 behind the goalkeeping of captain Gianpiero Combi, one of the best in the world at his position at the time.

Italian players carry manager Vittorio Pozzo
onto the pitch after winning the 1934 World Cup in Rome

# WORLD CUP HISTORY

1930
Host – Uruguay
Champion – Uruguay
Participants – 13
Leading Scorer –
   Guillermo Stábile (ARG)
Total Attendance –
   434,000

1950
Host – Brazil
Champion – Uruguay
Participants – 13
Leading Scorer –
   Ademir (BRA)
Total Attendance –
   1,337,000

1962
Host – Chile
Champion – Brazil
Participants – 16
Leading Scorer –
   Garrincha (BRA)
Total Attendance –
   776,000

1970
Host – Mexico
Champion – Brazil
Participants – 16
Leading Scorer –
   Gerd Müller (GER)
Total Attendance –
   1,673,975

1930	1940	1950	1960	1970

1934
Host – Italy
Champion – Italy
Participants – 16
Leading Scorer –
   Oldřich Nejedlý (CZE)
Total Attendance –
   395,000

1954
Host – Switzerland
Champion – West Germany
Participants – 16
Leading Scorer –
   Sándor Kocsis (HUN)
Total Attendance –
   943,000

1966
Host – England
Champion – England
Participants – 16
Leading Scorer –
   Eusébio (POR)
Total Attendance –
   1,614,677

1974
Host – West Germany
Champion – West Germany
Participants – 16
Leading Scorer –
   Grzegorz Lato (POL)
Total Attendance –
   1,774,022

1938
Host – France
Champion – Italy
Participants – 15
Leading Scorer –
   Leônidas da Silva (BRA)
Total Attendance –
   483,000

1958
Host – Sweden
Champion – Brazil
Participants – 16
Leading Scorer –
   Just Fontaine (FRA)
Total Attendance –
   868,000

1978
Host – Argentina
Champion – Argentina
Participants – 16
Leading Scorer –
   Mario Kempes (ARG)
Total Attendance –
   1,610,215

 The World Cup was not held in 1942 or 1946 due to World War II

1982
Host – Spain
Champion – Italy
Participants – 24
Leading Scorer –
Paolo Rossi (ITA)
Total Attendance –
1,856,277

1990
Host – Italy
Champion – West Germany
Participants – 24
Leading Scorer –
Salvatore Schillaci (ITA)
Total Attendance –
2,527,348

2002
Host – Japan/South Korea
Champion – Brazil
Participants – 32
Leading Scorer –
Ronaldo (BRA)
Total Attendance –
2,724,604

2010
Host – South Africa
Champion – Spain
Participants – 32
Leading Scorer –
Diego Forlán (URU)
Total Attendance –
3,167,984

1980   1990   2000   2010

1986
Host – Mexico
Champion – Brazil
Participants – 24
Leading Scorer –
Gary Lineker (ENG)
Total Attendance –
2,407,431

1994
Host – United States
Champion – Brazil
Participants – 24
Leading Scorer –
Hristo Stoichov (BUL)
Total Attendance –
3,586,567

2006
Host – Germany
Champion – Italy
Participants – 32
Leading Scorer –
Miroslav Klose (GER)
Total Attendance –
3,367,000

2014
Host – Brazil
Champion – Germany
Participants – 32
Leading Scorer –
James Rodríguez (COL)
Total Attendance –
3,429,873

1998
Host – France
Champion – France
Participants – 32
Leading Scorer –
Davor Šuker (CRO)
Total Attendance –
2,859,234

In the other semifinal, the former Czechoslovakia had a much easier time with Germany. This was due mostly to the play of Czechoslovakia's star forward Oldřich Nejedlý. Nejedlý had already scored two goals in the previous two matches and was in top form for this semifinal match. He scored a hat trick against the Germans, including the match winner with 20 minutes remaining.

The 1934 World Cup final was played in front of more than 50,000 fans in Rome, almost all of whom were rooting for the home team. Temperatures on that June day soared to more than 100 degrees Fahrenheit. Neither team scored in the first half. It was the Czechoslovakians who struck first, midway through the second half with a goal from winger Antonín Puč. Italian winger Raimundo Orsi scored to tie the match just 10 minutes later, however, and the match went to extra time. Italian striker Angelo Schiavo wasted little time, scoring his fourth goal of the tournament just five minutes into the extra time period. That was enough as Italy won 2–1 to give host nations a 2–0 record in World Cups.

 ## SIDEBAR: SILVIO PIOLA

One of the great players in the history of Italian soccer, Silvio Piola was the star of the 1938 World Cup for his victorious country, scoring five times in four matches. Piola would go on to score 30 goals in just 34 caps for Italy, but his brilliance extended beyond the international pitch.

Piola is the all-time leading scorer in the history of Serie A, the top league in Italy, where he potted 274 goals in 537 matches. Piola played primarily at Lazio, but ended his long career with seven seasons at Novara Calcio. The stadium there was named after him following his death in 1996 at age 83. No Italian goal scorer was more prolific than the Legend of Calcio.

1938 World Cup

As great as the expectation was that Europe would host the 1934 event, it was even more expected by South Americans that the event would **revert** to a South American host in 1938. France, Argentina, and Germany all submitted bids. Unsurprisingly, Germany, which was then under Nazi rule, received no votes to be host. Therefore it came as a shock to South Americans when Argentina received just four votes and lost the bid to France by a wide margin. Shock turned to insult and Argentina decided to **boycott** the 1938 World Cup. Similarly, 1930 host and champion Uruguay also refused to attend, joining Argentina on the sidelines.

Check out this short recap of the 1938 World Cup final

Under a new rule that year, Italy, as defending champions, and France, as host, were each given an automatic qualification. Europe was given 11 of the open qualifying slots, with two to the Americas and one to Asia. For the first time, the USA did not qualify a team, with Cuba earning the spot instead.

This was the first World Cup where world politics directly affected play and match outcomes, as it took place during the run-up to World War II. Austria and Germany had each qualified teams for the tournament, but just weeks before it began, the two countries merged, with Austria coming under Nazi control. As a result, the Nazis decided to enter only one team, under the German flag, consisting of both German and Austrian players. Therefore, only 15 teams took part in the 1938 World Cup.

The star of the 1938 World Cup for champion Italy, Silvio Piola has a stadium named for him in Vercelli

The 1938 tournament was also a straight knockout format. This meant that Sweden, Austria's scheduled opponent in the first round, advanced automatically. Most of the other teams had a much tougher time. Five of the first-round matches went to extra time, and two of those ended up needing to be replayed.

Defending champion Italy was among those taken to extra time in the first round, needing a goal four minutes into the extra period from striker Silvio Piola to win 2–1. Italy's second-round opponent was host France, who had beaten Belgium to open the tournament. Two second-half goals by Piola helped give Italy a 3–1 win, marking the first time a host nation had ever lost or been eliminated from the World Cup.

The former Czechoslovakia and the Netherlands meet
to play a first-round match at the 1938 World Cup

Next up for Italy in the semifinals was seven-goal scorer Leônidas da Silva and Brazil, who had beaten Nejedlý and Czechoslovakia in the previous round. After a goalless first half, the Italians broke free with a goal from striker Gino Colaussi six minutes into the second half, and held on to win 2–1.

For the final in Paris, the challenger to Italy's crown as world champions was Hungary. Each team scored in the first 10 minutes, but gradually, Piola and Colaussi took control of the match. Colaussi had two first-half goals and Piola had one, giving the Italians a 3–1 halftime lead. Piola scored his fifth goal of the tournament late in the half to secure a 4–2 win. Italy was the first team to defend the World Cup championship.

TEXT-DEPENDENT QUESTIONS:

1. What were the founding countries of FIFA?
2. What was the nickname of the 1934 Austrian national team?
3. How many goals did Italy's Silvio Piola score at the 1938 World Cup?

RESEARCH PROJECT:

Look up the 1934 Austrian national team and write a brief report on it. Detail the best players and their statistics, the accomplishments that made the team stand out, and what happened to the team after their failure in the World Cup.

WORDS TO UNDERSTAND:

corralled: collected or gathered

fearsome: causing awe or respect

sporadic: appearing or happening at irregular intervals in time; occasional

CHAPTER 2

THE WORLD CUP FINDS ITS LEGS (1950–66)

In 1939, tensions between Nazi Germany and the rest of Europe erupted into Word War II. With Europe transformed into a large-scale battlefield, the 1942 World Cup was cancelled. Although the war in Europe ended with Germany's surrender in May of 1945, there was no time to organize a soccer tournament, and most countries were in no position to do so, which meant there was no World Cup in 1946.

1950 World Cup

In the postwar period, finding a country with the available resources to host a World Cup was a challenge for Rimet and FIFA. Europe was almost certainly not an option. In the end, Brazil, which had prepared a bid for the 1942 event, stepped up and presented the only offer to host the next event. FIFA had little choice but to quickly take them up on their offer.

The staging of qualification matches was **sporadic** and challenging. Many countries had trouble assembling the resources to field a team. Countries such as Bolivia, Chile, India, Paraguay, Switzerland, and Turkey all qualified by default. Turkey and India later pulled out, claiming financial hardship. France, which had been eliminated in qualifying, agreed to fill an available slot, but it also pulled out just before the tournament.

Ultimately, just 13 teams took part in the 1950 World Cup, including the USA. It would be the last time the USA qualified a team for 40 years. Brazilian organizers insisted on switching to a round-robin format to guarantee more matches, and therefore generate more match revenue. The teams were drawn into four groups of four, but due to late withdrawals, one group had just two teams, and another had only three. After the first round-robin, the four group winners advanced to a final four-team round-robin group stage, with the final group winner declared the champion.

Maracanã Stadium, site of several matches during the 1950 World Cup, including the stunning 2–1 upset of the host Brazil by Uruguay in the final

The round one group winners were Spain, Sweden, Uruguay, and host Brazil. On the last day of the final-stage round-robin between these four teams, Sweden played Spain and Uruguay faced Brazil. The points standings were: Brazil – 4, Uruguay – 3, Spain – 1, Sweden – 0. This meant that no matter what happened, the winner of the Brazil vs. Uruguay match would win the World Cup (in the event of a draw, Brazil would win). The Brazilians were heavily favored in front of their home fans. A Uruguay win was considered so unlikely that Rimet only wrote a speech congratulating Brazil, and the winner's medals were engraved ahead of time with the names of the Brazilian players.

Led by Ademir, who came in to the final with eight tournament goals, Brazil attacked throughout the match. The Brazilians finally managed a goal just two minutes into the second half to take a 1–0 lead. Undaunted, Uruguay fought back, and shocked the Brazilians by scoring the equalizer 20 minutes later. When winger Alcides Ghiggia scored the final goal for Uruguay, the crowd sat in stunned silence as Uruguay claimed another World Cup championship. In Brazil, the match result is considered a national tragedy dubbed the Maracanzo, named after Maracanã Stadium, where the match was played.

SIDEBAR: GIANT KILLERS

At the 1950 World Cup, England was the heavy favorite to advance. This was the first World Cup appearance for England, as all the British nations (England, Ireland, Scotland, and Wales) had withdrawn from FIFA in 1928 and had been ineligible to participate until they rejoined the association immediately after the war. The English showed their strength in their opening match against Chile, winning 2–0. The other teams in the group were Spain and the USA, and England played the Americans in their second match.

Expectations were that England would destroy the United States. The English players were some of the best professionals in the world, whereas the Americans were a collection of semi-pro players who worked primarily as dishwashers, school teachers, hearse drivers, and the like. England was so confident of victory that its best player, Stanley Matthews, did not even play in the match. Even American coach Bill Jeffrey anticipated a slaughter.

As the match began, it quickly became clear that the only real challenge for the English would be American goalkeeper Frank Borghi. Half an hour into the match, Borghi had already made three standout saves. Then disaster struck for England. On an easy shot from 25 yards out, English goalkeeper Bert Williams moved to catch the ball. However, American center forward Joe Gaetjens dove forward and just got his head on the ball, right before it reached Williams. The ball deflected away from the keeper and into the net for an unexpected American goal.

Borghi continued to play brilliantly in the second half, including a match-saving stop in the 82nd minute. The USA held on for a shocking 1–0 win. It was the only win of the tournament for the Americans, but it was a memorable achievement. For the English, it was a devastating loss from which they could not recover. They were eliminated after losing the next match to Spain.

Hungary's Golden Team, led by superstar Ferenc Puskás (front row, center), was the heavy favorite to win the 1954 World Cup as they came in on a 31-match-win streak

1954 World Cup

Switzerland was the only nation to bid for hosting the 1954 World Cup. With four more years of distance from the war, 16 teams again participated, and the format consisted of a group stage followed by a knockout stage. The unusual element in that year's format was that the group stage was not a round-robin. Even though there were four teams in each group, each team was scheduled to play only two matches, rather than three. Germany, banned from competing in 1950, qualified as West Germany, since the former country was now politically separated into two nations.

West Germany was one of the countries to advance to the knockout stage, where it beat Yugoslavia 2–0 in the quarterfinals. Also advancing to the semifinals was defending champion Uruguay, who beat England 4–2. Uruguay lost 4–2 in its semifinal to Hungary, but this was not an upset. Nicknamed "The Golden Team," the Hungarians were the top team in the world at the time. They entered the World Cup having won 31 straight matches, and were heavily favored to win the tournament.

West Germany beat Austria handily to advance to the final in the city of Bern against Hungary. As in 1950, everyone expected a blowout, but just like in the Maracanazo, the underdog had other ideas. The Hungarians came out in **fearsome** fashion, led by Sándor Kocsis and superstar striker Ferenc Puskás, who scored six minutes in. Hungary added another goal two minutes later and it appeared the rout was on. West Germany, however, refused to be intimidated, and scored two goals of its own in the next 10 minutes. After four goals in 18 minutes, the match settled down. No more goals were scored until just six minutes remained in the match. That is when West German forward Helmut Rahn intercepted a short clearing attempt near the top of the box and struck a low shot past the Hungarian keeper for his second goal of the match and one of the biggest upsets in World Cup history. In Germany, the match is known as the Miracle at Bern.

1958 World Cup

Sweden was the only country to enter a bid to host the 1958 tournament. Aside from Sweden and West Germany, spots were allocated as follows: **Europe (UEFA) – 8, South America (CONMEBOL) – 3, North America (CONCACAF) – 2, Asia/Africa (AFC/CAF) – 1**.

The tournament featured a group stage (with a full round-robin) followed by a knockout stage. The top two teams in each of four groups of four teams advanced. The 1958 event is notable as the World Cup debut of Brazil's Pelé, just 17 years old at the time. Regarded as the best ever to play the sport, the Brazilian teenager made his mark at this tournament.

Pelé scored the only goal of the match in the first knockout contest, a 1–0 quarterfinal win over Wales. Next came the French in the semifinals, and Pelé blasted them, scoring a second-half hat trick in a 5–2 win. In the final match, Brazil met the host Swedes. Pelé was again merciless. With Brazil leading 2–1 in the second half, he scored 10 minutes in to crush the hopes of the Swedes, then scored a second goal at the very end of the half to salt away a 5–2 win and Brazil's first title.

1962 World Cup

Chile was selected over Argentina as the host for the 1962 World Cup. Qualifying was used to trim 57 interested member nations down to the required 16. Compared to the previous tournament, the CONCACAF,

AFC, and CAF spots became playoff spots rather than guaranteed entries. The winners in these regions then played playoff matches against European teams to receive a spot. As a result, the 1962 tournament featured 10 UEFA teams, 5 from CONMEBOL (including the hosts and champions), and Mexico.

The defending champions got off to a fast start as Pelé scored in the first group-stage match, a 2–0 win for Brazil over Mexico. By 1962, Pelé was universally regarded as the best player in the world, but the superstar was injured badly enough in the next match that he missed the rest of the tournament. That match ended in a draw, but even without Pelé, Brazil was still able to beat Spain next to win its group and advance. Pelé's replacement, Amarildo, scored twice in that match.

The hero of the 1962 World Cup, Garrincha is a legend in Brazil, as this street art homage in São Paulo demonstrates

The player who really stepped up for Brazil while Pelé was unavailable was the winger known as Garrincha. In the first knockout-round match against England, Garrincha collected two goals in a 3–1 win, and then scored two more in the 4–2 semifinals win over host Chile. The final brought a rematch against group-stage companions Czechoslovakia. The Czechoslovakians scored early, but Amarildo equalized quickly and the match was tied at halftime. Zito scored for Brazil midway through the second half, and Vavá scored his fourth of the tournament late to cap a 3–1 win and claim back-to-back World Cup titles.

1966 World Cup

England beat out competing bids from Spain and West Germany to host the 1966 World Cup. African members boycotted this tournament to protest FIFA's refusal to guarantee an African team a spot rather than forcing CAF champions to win a playoff to qualify.

English goalkeeper Gordon Banks got the hosts off to a perfect start as he did not concede a goal in the first four matches to lead England to the semifinals against Portugal. Superstar striker Eusébio led the Portuguese. In the quarterfinal against North Korea, Eusébio scored four goals. English midfielder Bobby Charlton, however, would not be overshadowed, scoring once in the first half and again in the second half in the match against Portugal. England's defense, led by captain center back Bobby Moore, kept Eusébio in check throughout the match. The Portuguese star would finally beat Banks on a late penalty kick, but it was too little too late, and England advanced 2–1.

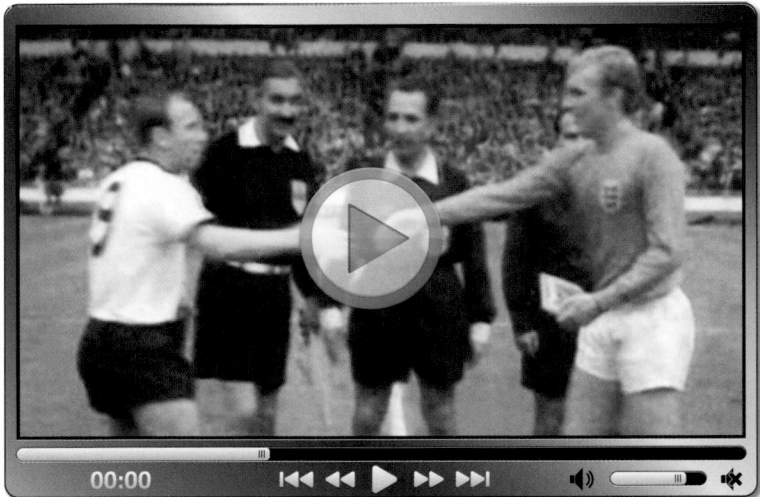

Watch the highlights of the England-West Germany final from the 1966 World Cup

In the final against West Germany, the story was England center forward Geoff Hurst. Defensive stalwart Franz Beckenbauer anchored the Germans at midfield, and England had yet to concede anything other than a penalty kick, but this match belonged to the men up front.

West Germany scored first, beating Banks for the first time off a failed clearance. Hurst drew England level just seven minutes later by heading in a perfectly placed Moore free kick. The score was 1–1 at the half. It remained that way until late in the second half, when Hurst proved dangerous again. Off a corner kick this time, Hurst fired a shot from the top of the 18-yard box that deflected off a defender to teammate Martin Peters, who buried the goal. With less than two minutes remaining, the referee awarded West Germany a free kick that was one to remember. The kick struck the wall of English defenders lined up 10 yards away.

Geoff Hurst, memorialized here in this statue of the 1966 World Cup champions with Bobby Moore sitting on his left shoulder, is revered as a hero in England because of his hat trick in the final against West Germany

A German player **corralled** the loose ball and fired another shot, which hit one of his own players in front of the English goal. It bounced across the goalmouth to Wolfgang Weber, who blasted it past a scrambling Banks for the equalizer.

The match went to extra time, during which Hurst was dominant. Eleven minutes in, he trapped a cross from Allan Ball at the edge of the six-yard box with his back to goal. He moved to his left, spun, and fired a hard shot over the keeper that hit the underside of the crossbar and bounced down to land just over the goal line. The referee needed to consult the linesman to confirm the ball was indeed over the line. Hurst completed a hat trick and the 4–2 win with a goal in the last minute to give England its first and only World Cup championship.

Queen Elizabeth II presents the trophy to Bobby Moore, captain of host champions England at the 1966 World Cup

TEXT-DEPENDENT QUESTIONS:

1. How many World Cups were cancelled due to World War II, and in which years would they have been held?
2. Which country hosted the 1954 World Cup?
3. How many goals did Geoff Hurst score in the 1966 World Cup final match?

RESEARCH PROJECT:

The 1966 World Cup is the only one that England has won. As the nation that invented the sport, the English take great pride in that victory and their countrymen hold the players from that team in high regard. Research the players from the 1966 World Cup champions, then pick three who have been honored for their accomplishments and write a one-page report on each.

WORDS TO UNDERSTAND:

complements: things that complete something else or make it better

deke: a fake or feint intended to deceive a defensive player, often drawing that player out of position

unorthodox: not conforming to rules, traditions, or modes of conduct

CHAPTER 3

FROM THE FEET OF PELÉ TO THE HAND OF GOD (1970–86)

The first eight FIFA World Cup tournaments had all been held in either Europe (five times) or South America (three times). So it was a sign of the global growth of the sport when Mexico was chosen in 1964 as host for the 1970 World Cup, and beat out a competing bid from Argentina. Mexico had proved itself over the years, qualifying for every World Cup since World War II (it would qualify in 1966 as well). FIFA recognized this by granting Mexico the first World Cup outside Europe or South America.

1970 World Cup

After the boycott in 1966, African (Confédération Africaine de Football, CAF) teams were guaranteed a spot in the 1970 World Cup, and Morocco appeared in the tournament for the first time. Other first-time participants included Israel and El Salvador. However, this World Cup would not be about the new teams. Instead, a very familiar team led by one of the most famous athletes in the world took center stage.

The team that represented Brazil at the 1970 World Cup is believed by many to have been the best team ever assembled. Pelé was still near the height of his greatness, but this team had plenty of star power throughout the roster. Captain Carlos Alberto patrolled the defense from right back.

Rivellino (center) and Jairzinho (standing at right) were two of the key players who, along with Pelé, led Brazil to the 1970 World Cup title

Gérson anchored the midfield. Up front, Jairzinho, Rivellino, and Tostão were formidable **complements** to Pelé. Jairzinho and Tostão are, along with Pelé, among the top-ten goal scorers in Brazil national team history.

As expected, Brazil swept undefeated through the group stage behind three goals from Pelé and four from Jairzinho in three matches. In the knockout stage, the quarterfinal victim was Peru, which lost 4–2 on goals from Jairzinho, Rivellino, and a pair from Tostão. In the semifinal match against Uruguay, Jairzinho and Rivellino each had second-half goals in a 3–1 Brazil win. The final pitted the Brazilians against a good defending Italian side, but Brazil's quality was just too much. Pelé opened the scoring, but Italy managed to equalize before halftime, and it was 1–1 to start the second. The Brazilian attack, however, came in waves in the final 45 minutes. First it was Gérson, then five minutes later Jairzinho scored, and then four minutes from the end, Carlos Alberto made it 4–1. Carlos Alberto's goal is considered to be one of the greatest examples of team skill ever at the World Cup. Brazil easily won its third title.

An extraordinary display of skill and teamwork leads to a perfect Brazilian goal at the 1970 World Cup

1974 World Cup

West Germany was the site for the 1974 World Cup. Defending champions Brazil would be a factor, but with Pelé now retired from international competition, its best days had passed. By contrast, Beckenbauer and the host team, with veteran striker Gerd Müller in top form, would be up to the challenge. Perhaps the team most of the world looked forward to watching was the Netherlands, led by dynamic captain Johan Cruyff.

SIDEBAR: THE GREAT EIGHT

Through twenty World Cup tournaments from 1930 to 2014, only eight countries have seen their team's players hoist the champion's trophy. In all, 77 countries have qualified teams over the decades, but only these eight have managed to outlast all others to claim victory in the sport's ultimate competition.

Brazil (5) 1958, 1962, 1970, 1994, 2002
Italy (4) 1934, 1938, 1982, 2006
Germany (4) 1954, 1974, 1990, 2014
Argentina (2) 1978, 1986
Uruguay (2) 1930, 1950
England 1966
France 1998
Spain 2010

The format changed for this World Cup, reverting back to one like that at the 1958 tournament. The knockout stage was eliminated and instead the top-two sides from each group in the first round advanced to a second round-robin group stage with two groups of four. The winners of each of these groups played in the final match.

As expected, the Netherlands, West Germany, and Brazil all advanced to the second group stage. Both second-stage groups came down to what were essentially semifinal matches. On the last day of the second-stage matches, Brazil played the Netherlands to decide Group A, and West Germany played Grzegorz Lato and his Polish team to decide Group B. In front of 62,000 fans in Frankfurt, Poland gave the Germans a tough test. West Germany finally prevailed 1–0 on a late goal by Müller.

Over in Group A, the Dutch had continued to work their "Total Football" system to perfection. It was an **unorthodox** system in which any player could move to fill the position of any other teammate, making it just as

Netherlands captain Johan Cruyff (first from the left, in orange) led the Dutch in their Total Football system to the 1974 World Cup final. Here they are just minutes from the start of a 2–0 second-round win over East Germany

likely for any player to create plays, score goals, or defend. Going into the final match of the second group stage, it had worked so well that no team had yet scored against the Dutch, while they themselves had scored 12 goals in five matches. Brazil had no better luck than previous Dutch opponents, coming up empty in a 2–0 loss.

In the final against West Germany, the Dutch struck quickly as Cruyff was fouled in the penalty area in the 2nd minute of the match. The Dutch converted the penalty to lead 1–0, but the Germans were awarded a penalty of their own 23 minutes later to level the match. West Germany then scored a crucial goal two minutes before the half. A brilliant run down the right side by midfielder Rainer Bonhof was rewarded despite his short pass to the middle being behind Müller. Müller stopped, took a step back, and turned and shot in the same motion, taking the Dutch keeper by surprise. The shot went in, and the first breakdown of the Total Football system proved to be the World Cup winner for West Germany's second title.

1978 World Cup

Argentina was host to the 1978 World Cup, which was played under the same format used in 1974. The Netherlands was back and still in good form despite the retirement of Cruyff from international play. The Brazilians were strong as always, but there was also plenty of optimism around the host side, La Albiceleste (Argentina's team nickname, meaning "the white and sky blue" after their uniform colors).

Johan Neeskens of the Netherlands fires the ball past a sliding Franz Beckenbauer of West Germany in a desperate attempt to score the equalizer in the 1974 World Cup final. West Germany held on to win 2–1

Argentina and Italy both survived a tough Group 1 in the opening stage, where Italy went undefeated and Argentina's only loss came to the Italians. In the second round, they were in opposite groups, with Italy in with the Netherlands in Group A and Argentina grouped with Brazil in Group B.

In Group A, Italy and the Netherlands met in the final match of the second stage. Each team had three points, but the Netherlands had a better goal differential, so it needed only a draw to win the group. Italy had to win, but came up short, losing 2–1.

In Group B, the situation was more complicated. Argentina and Brazil were atop the group with three points each, but were not playing each other in the last match. Brazil had Poland, while Argentina faced Peru. Brazil had a +3 goal differential, with Argentina at +2. So Argentina needed to beat Peru by two more goals than Brazil beat Poland. The matches kicked off simultaneously. Brazil won 3–0, but Argentina won 6–0 to claim the group.

Argentina's Mario Kempes celebrates the tournament-winning goal against the Netherlands at the 1978 World Cup

This set up a Netherlands-Argentina final. Argentina's Mario Kempes was the hot player coming in. He did not score in the first group stage, but had scored four of the last eight Argentina goals. In the final, Kempes did not disappoint. The attacking midfielder opened the scoring seven minutes from halftime, a lead which Argentina held until the Dutch finally scored with eight minutes left in the match. In extra time, Kempes was the hero. Halfway into the period, he broke in alone on the Dutch keeper, who rushed at him at the top of the six-yard box. Kempes's shot was saved by the keeper's left hand, then went off Kempes's right shin as he leapt over the sprawling keeper. The ball then hit the keeper in the head and bounced to Kempes near the left post, and he managed to get the spikes of his outstretched right foot on the ball and knock it in before two onrushing Dutch defenders could clear it. The stadium erupted, and Argentina went on to win 3–1 for its first title.

1982 World Cup

The 1982 World Cup in Spain was all about Italy's Paolo Rossi. Yes, there was a significant format change, as the tournament expanded for the first time to include 24 teams. This meant the first round had six groups of four teams, but still with two teams advancing from each group. The second round then had four groups of three teams. Both group stages were round-robins, and the group winners in stage two advanced to the semifinals. As it turned out, Rossi did not make his presence felt until the second match in the second round.

Italy had advanced to the second round without the benefit of a win, achieving three first-round draws. It then beat Argentina 2–1 in the first second-round match, giving it just four goals in four matches. In the next match, against Brazil, Rossi scored three all by himself. The veteran striker scored two in the first half, but Brazil equalized at 68 minutes. Holding the tiebreaker, the Brazilians only needed a draw. Six minutes later, Rossi scored again off a botched clearance of a corner kick to send Italy to the semifinals.

In the semifinals against Poland, Rossi was superb again, scoring both Italy goals in a 2–0 win. In the final against West Germany, 90,000 fans in Madrid watched a goalless first half, but then Rossi gave them what they came to see 17 minutes into the second half. Teammate Claudio

The Spanish government minted a special five peseta coin to commemorate the country's hosting of the 1982 World Cup

Gentile bounced in a cross from the right side that Rossi got his head on to knock it past the keeper for his sixth goal of the tournament. He was named Golden Ball and Golden Boot winner as Italy won World Cup trophy number three.

1986 World Cup

What Rossi was to 1982, Argentina's Diego Maradona was to 1986. Maradona came into the tournament in Mexico regarded as the best player in the world by most, so, unlike Rossi, he was expected to dominate. The young superstar had a fiery reputation, which grew a thousand times over after the 1986 World Cup.

With a change made to have 16 of the 24 teams advance out of the first round, Argentina barely had to try to move forward, easily winning its round one group with just a single goal contributed by Maradona. In the round of 16 knockout stage, Argentina beat Uruguay 1–0 to advance to the quarterfinals against England. It was there that Maradona cemented his legend.

The match against a quality English side was 0–0 early in the second half when Maradona struck twice in extraordinary fashion. In the 51st minute, Maradona drove the middle against the English defense, beating three defenders before passing to his right at the top of the box and running directly at the goal, expecting the one-two pass. The ball was deflected by a defender, however, and popped up high in the air. Maradona and the keeper both jumped for the ball, and it hit Maradona and went in. The English defense screamed for a hand ball call, but none came, and the goal stood. Replays showed the ball hitting his hand, which was up above his head, but it was 1–0 Argentina.

Argentina, led by the incomparable Diego Maradona, was World Cup champion in 1986 after defeating Germany 3–2

Diego Maradona leaves English defenders in his wake seconds before scoring the Goal of the Century at the 1986 World Cup

Just four minutes later, Maradona scorched the shell-shocked English defense again with the Goal of the Century. He got the ball at midfield, where he beat two defenders and started a run dribbling down the right side. He cut to the inside, beating two more defenders as he broke into the penalty area. Maradona took one more touch to **deke** the onrushing keeper to his right and tapped the ball into the vacant goal with his left foot. La Albiceleste held on for the 2–1 win.

Maradona would add two more goals in a 2–0 semifinal win over Belgium. In the final, he did not score, but did set up the World Cup-winning goal by Jorge Burruchaga with a brilliant one-touch pass. It was Argentina's second World Cup championship.

TEXT-DEPENDENT QUESTIONS:

1. In which two years has Mexico hosted the World Cup?
2. How many goals did Mario Kempes score at the 1978 World Cup?
3. Who scored the World Cup-winning goal for Argentina in 1986?

RESEARCH PROJECT:

Compare and contrast the careers of Pelé and Diego Maradona. Report their playing statistics and discuss their playing styles. How were they similar? What made each player most distinct? Write an opinion on their legacies to the sport in their own countries, and to the sport as a whole.

WORDS TO UNDERSTAND:

indicative: pointing out or showing something

lackluster: without excitement or interest

stalemate: a contest, dispute, competition, etc., in which neither side can gain an advantage or win

AFRICA, ASIA, AND EXPANDING THE FIELD (1990–2006)

With the expansion of the World Cup field to 24 teams in 1982, there were more spots to be filled. The confederation that benefitted most from the expansion was UEFA, as Europe was allocated five of the eight new spots. The other five confederations got no more than one spot each, if any. The CAF, for example had nearly as many members as UEFA, yet Africa had only two spots. The push for FIFA to be more inclusive of the other confederations would continue into the 1990s.

1990 World Cup

Italy was the site of the 1990 World Cup, 56 years after it first hosted the event. This tournament was notable for bringing African soccer to the forefront thanks to a remarkable result by Cameroon. Cameroon had previously qualified in 1982, but that side had failed to win a match and scored only a single goal. In 1990, however, things were very different.

The Indomitable Lions, as the Cameroonian team is nicknamed, drew into a group with Romania, the Soviet Union, and defending champions Argentina. Cameroon opened against Diego Maradona and Argentina, but was not intimidated by the champions or the spotlight. Cameroon played a rough defensive style and was shown five cards by the referee during the match. One of its midfielders was sent off after a red card on a vicious tackle in the middle of the second half. Undaunted, the Lions scored just six minutes later and held on for the 1–0 win. A 2–1 win over Romania behind a pair of goals from 38-year-old substitute Roger Milla in the team's second match guaranteed that Cameroon would advance.

Milla would be the hero against Colombia in the first match of the knockout rounds as well. Again, coming on as a second-half substitute, Milla ended up scoring twice within two minutes in extra time to give Cameroon a 2–0 lead that turned into a 2–1 win. Cameroon's great run came to an end in the quarterfinals against England, but the Lions did not go quietly. They scored two goals four minutes apart in the second half to take a 2–1 lead with 25 minutes left. Fouls would prove to be Cameroon's downfall, however, as they conceded two penalty kicks, one late in regulation and the other in extra time. England's Gary Lineker converted both to secure a 3–2 win.

No African nation had ever advanced to the quarterfinals at the World Cup. The 1990 World Cup was the most watched of all World Cups to date, so much of the world saw the quality that a well-coached African team could bring—a realization that would have a significant future impact. However, at that moment in time, it was more of the same on the pitch, as other former champions West Germany, Argentina, and Italy joined England in the semifinals. For the second straight World Cup, West Germany faced Argentina in the final. This time, West Germany won 1–0.

There was no divine intervention for Maradona and Argentina in 1990, as they lost the final rematch 1–0 to West Germany

Cameroon and Roger Milla were the story of the 1990 World Cup, pushing African soccer into the global spotlight with a quarterfinals run

SIDEBAR: AMERICA IS ABOVE AVERAGE

When the bid from the United States was awarded the 1994 World Cup, there was criticism of its selection. The general sentiment was that the USA did not deserve the privilege of hosting as it generally cared little, and knew even less, about the sport. As University of Michigan professor Andrei Markovits expressed in his book *Offside: Soccer and American Exceptionalism*, "We were always laughed at for not playing the world's game, that we were outsiders and so on, and we couldn't do anything right." When the time came to play the matches however, Americans showed that they will always turn out for a big event, even if it is not traditionally or culturally their own.

Here are the top ten World Cups in order of all-time average attendance per match—the USA in 1994 has been tops for 20 years.

WORLD CUP	TOTAL ATTENDANCE	AVERAGE ATTENDANCE
1994 USA	3,568,567	68,626
1950 Brazil	1,337,000	60,773
2014 Brazil	3,429,873	53,592
2006 Germany	3,367,000	52,609
1970 Mexico	1,673,975	52,312
1966 England	1,614,677	50,459
2010 South Africa	3,167,984	49,499
1990 Italy	2,527,348	48,411
1986 Mexico	2,407,431	46,297
1974 Germany	1,774,022	46,685

1994 World Cup

The impact of Cameroon's great showing in 1990 was reflected in the allocation of spots for the 1994 World Cup in the United States. A qualifying spot that had been allotted to Europe in the 1990 expansion was given to Africa for 1994. That meant Cameroon, Morocco, and Nigeria qualified for the 1994 tournament, the most teams to ever represent Africa at a World Cup.

Neither African team matched the 1990 success of Cameroon. Instead, the story on the pitch was a familiar one, authored by an artist in yellow and blue named Romário. Romário was the latest superstar Brazilian striker, and he led his team undefeated through the group stage by scoring in all three group matches.

In the round of 16, Brazil faced the United States. The Americans played a very competitive match in front of more than 84,000 fans in Stanford, California. Brazil needed a late goal from Bebeto to win 1–0. In the quarterfinals against the Netherlands, second-half goals from Romário and Bebeto put Brazil up 2–0 with 27 minutes to play. The scoring, however, had just begun. The Dutch tied the match up in 13 minutes, until defender Branco scored for Brazil with 9 minutes on the clock. In a wild match that saw five goals in 28 minutes, Brazil held on to win 3–2. In the semifinal match against Sweden, Romário was the hero late as he scored with just 10 minutes left to secure a 1–0 Brazil win.

The final against Italy pitted a pair of three-time champions against each other in a rematch of the 1970 final. The match took place at the Rose Bowl stadium in Pasadena, California, with more than 94,000 in attendance. This crowd was **indicative** of the great success of the tournament. The 1994 event continues to hold the record for the highest total attendance in World Cup history. The crowd that night witnessed a tight defensive struggle with few chances in regulation or extra time.

With the score 0–0, the final was decided by a penalty kick shootout. Italy's Franco Baresi sent the first penalty kick over the bar, but Pagliuca bailed him out by saving the next kick by Brazil's Márcio Santos. Each team made its next two penalties, making it 2–2 after three of five attempts. Italy's Daniele Massaro was up next, but Brazil keeper Cláudio

Brazil beat Italy in a penalty kick shootout to win the 1994 World Cup final at the Rose Bowl Stadium in Pasadena, California

Taffarel guessed correctly, diving to his left to make the save. Brazil's Dunga scored to make it 4–3 after four attempts, which meant Italy had to score on its fifth attempt to stay alive. Star center forward Roberto Baggio took the penalty, but like Baresi, sailed the shot over the bar to give Brazil its fourth title.

Check out the highlights of the 1994 World Cup final between Italy and Brazil

1998 World Cup

The 1998 World Cup in France saw another expansion of the World Cup final field. Eight more spots were added, bringing the total number to 32. This included three from Asia, three from North America, four from South America, five from Africa, fourteen from Europe, and one playoff spot that went to either Asia or Oceania. This expansion allowed for the much sought-after addition of more teams from federations outside Europe and South America, especially from Asia and Africa, which both have large federation memberships.

Much like many previous World Cups, Brazil, Germany (East and West Germany had unified in 1990), and Italy came in as the favorites to win the tournament, ranked first, second, and third in the world at the time. The host French were the sixth-ranked European team and just 18th in the world, so not a lot was expected of them despite the fact that they had all-world midfielder Zinedine Zidane.

As expected, Brazil, Germany, and Italy all won their groups in the first round. With 32 teams, there were now eight groups of four teams, with the top two in each group advancing to the knockout stage. The French, however, also easily won their group. France was quite fortunate with the draw, with South Africa (24), Denmark (27) and Saudi Arabia (34), all ranked outside the top 20, ending with them in Group C. France did not lose a match, giving up just a single goal to the Danes.

The luck of the French continued in the round of 16, where their opponent was 29th-ranked Paraguay, runners up in a similarly weak Group D. Behind a third clean sheet from keeper Fabien Barthez, the French won 1–0 with a late goal in extra time. Brazil, Germany, and Italy all won their matches to advance to the quarterfinals as well, and it was the Italians who awaited France in the next round.

The two defense-minded sides played to a **stalemate** in regulation time, and it was more of the same in extra time, as Barthez's fourth clean sheet was matched by Pagliuca in the Italian goal. The match came down to a penalty kick shootout, where Italy's Luigi Di Biagio hit the crossbar on the final kick to eliminate his team.

In the other quarterfinal match on the same side of the draw with France, Croatia shocked Germany 3–0 to advance to the semifinals against the hosts. For the fifth time in six matches, the French faced a lower-ranked opponent. Following a goalless first half, striker Davor Šuker finally beat Barthez for just the second time in the tournament. Just one minute later, however, France equalized on a goal from right back Lilian Thuram. Then, in the 70th minute, Thuram struck again, hitting a left-footed blast from well out just inside the left post to secure a 2–1 win.

In the 1998 final against Ronaldo and Brazil, Zinedine Zidane and France won 3–0 to claim the first World Cup title for that country

Awaiting France and its delirious fans in the final was, as expected, top-ranked defending champions Brazil and superstar striker Ronaldo. It was France who came out aggressively, led by Zidane, who set up Stéphane Guivarc'h for a beautiful chance in the box early, and had a magnificent free kick headed over the bar by teammate Youri Djorkaeff. Barthez stopped two glorious Brazilian chances on his goal line before Zidane was finally rewarded in the 27th minute. Off a corner kick by Emmanuel Petit, Zidane outjumped the defender at the near post to head home the opening goal. With time waning in the first half, Zidane struck again, heading in another corner kick after his defender fell down and left him unmarked. Brazil pressed throughout the second half, but could not beat a determined Barthez, even after France went down to 10 men after center back Marcel Desailly was sent off following a second yellow card in the 68th minute. Petit scored a late goal to make the final 3–0 for the hosts and first-time winners.

HOSTS WITH THE MOST

URUGUAY

- 1930 Host & Champion
- 1930 population – 1,734,000
- Team captain – José Nasazzi
- World Cup-winning goal – Santos Iriarte
- Total goals scored – 15

ITALY

- 1934 Host & Champion
- 1934 population – 42,297,301
- Team captain – Gianpiero Combi
- World Cup-winning goal – Angelo Schiavio
- Total goals scored – 11

ENGLAND

- 1966 Host & Champion
- 1966 population – 42,309,869
- Team captain – Bobby Moore
- World Cup-winning goal – Geoff Hurst
- Total goals scored – 11

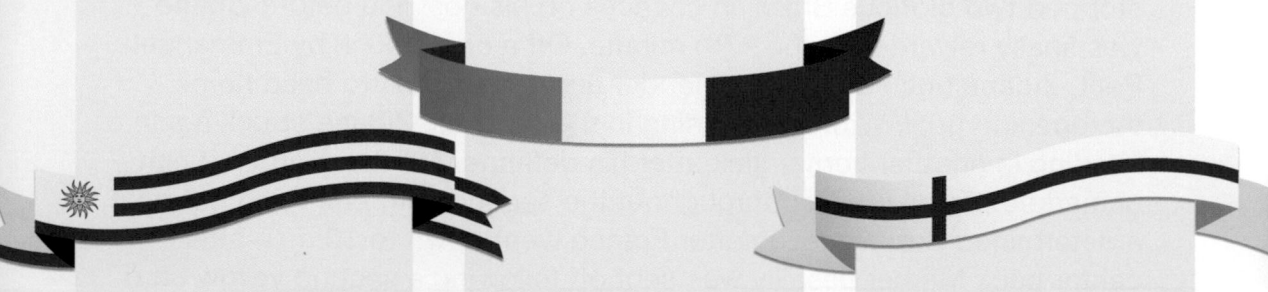

30% of World Cup host nations have won the trophy while hosting the world—that's six nations that have managed to give home fans the ultimate thrill

WEST GERMANY

- 1974 Host & Champion
- 1974 population – 61,991,500
- Team captain – Franz Beckenbauer
- World Cup-winning goal – Gerd Müller
- Total goals scored – 13

ARGENTINA

- 1978 Host & Champion
- 1978 population – 27,280,000
- Team captain – Daniel Passarella
- World Cup-winning goal – Mario Kempes
- Total goals scored – 15

FRANCE

- 1998 Host & Champion
- 1998 population – 60,190,000
- Team captain – Didier Deschamps
- World Cup-winning goal – Zinedine Zidane
- Total goals scored – 15

2002 World Cup

One of the reasons given for expanding to 32 teams in 1998 was to allow greater opportunity for teams from Asia and Africa to show how far they had come. In 2002, Asia was afforded another chance to shine as two of its member nations combined to be the first-ever joint hosts of a World Cup. The 2002 World Cup was hosted by both Japan and South Korea, and was the first to be held in Asia. The South Koreans and Japanese both qualified teams as hosts, but neither was expected to do well as both sides were ranked outside the top 30 in the world.

Two countries that were expected to dominate were the same two that played for the trophy in 1998: top-ranked France and second-ranked Brazil. The Brazilians breezed through Group C, winning all three matches. For the French, it was a different story in Group A— even though no other team in their group was ranked higher than 20th. France opened with a **lackluster** performance against 42nd-ranked Senegal, and lost 1–0. Next came Uruguay in a match where neither side could generate much of an attack. It ended in a 0–0 draw. This set up a must-win match against Denmark for France to advance. The French played their worst match, losing 2–0 and allowing Denmark to win the group. Senegal, the lowest-ranked African team in the competition, also advanced thanks to two draws and the win over France. The top-ranked, defending champion French went home in embarrassment, without having scored a goal. Due to this poor performance by the French, FIFA decided to revoke the automatic qualification of the defending champion for future World Cups. Now all teams but the hosts have to qualify.

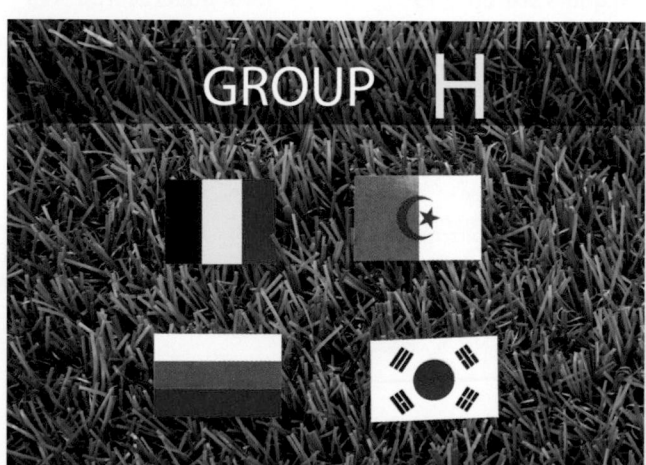

The host South Koreans were fortunate to draw into Group H with Belgium, Russia, and Tunisia, none of whom was ranked higher than 23rd in the world by FIFA for the 2002 World Cup

Seoul, South Korea, was one of the host cities for the 2002 World Cup

As for the 2002 hosts, both did amazingly well. In a relatively easy but competitive Group H with Belgium (ranked 23rd), Russia (28th), and Tunisia (31st), 32nd-ranked Japan played well. It opened with a draw against Belgium, then won its last two matches to claim the group. Over in Group D, the 40th-ranked South Koreans had it much tougher with Portugal (5th), USA (13th), and Poland (38th). The cohosts opened with a strong performance against Poland, winning 2–0 in what most experts thought would be their only victory. Next followed another strong performance against the USA in which the South Koreans managed to hold the Americans to a 1–1 draw. The powerful Portuguese were next. Portugal had avenged a 3–2 loss to the USA by pounding Poland 4–0. Portugal needed a win over South Korea to advance. The South Korean defense was stout, however, as it had been in every match. Portugal, which had scored 6 goals in two matches, could not beat keeper Lee Woon-jae, and a goal by the hosts in the 70th minute stood for the win.

Japan moved on to play Turkey after winning its group, and lost a close match 1–0 in the round of 16. South Korea faced 6th-ranked Italy and superstar goalkeeper Gianluigi Buffon. The referee awarded an early penalty kick to Korea when an Italian defender pulled an opponent down by the jersey in the box, but Buffon saved the penalty kick by diving to his right. The Italians then scored in the 18th minute, forcing South Korea to play catch up all match long. It appeared defeat was inevitable with just two minutes left. That is when defender Christian Panucci misplayed a chip into the box and deflected the ball right to the feet of Seol Ki-hyeon, who easily beat a helpless Buffon. The match went to extra time tied 1–1, where a controversial referee's decision to caution Italian midfielder Francesco Totti for embellishment resulted in Totti's dismissal. He had previously received a yellow card in the first half. Then 14 minutes later, with the Italians trying to hang on while playing with 10 men, their defense failed to cover Ahn Jung-hwan on the six-yard box, and he got his head on a cross to knock it in past Buffon for the match winner.

In South Korea's quarterfinal against eighth-ranked Spain, both keepers kept clean sheets through extra time, forcing a penalty kick shootout. The first six shooters all made their kicks, making it 3–3 with the fourth shooters coming up for each team. Ahn made his kick to put South Korea up 4–3. Joaquin was up next for Spain, but as he approached, Lee guessed correctly and dove to his left. Joaquin kicked it right at Lee for the save. Hong Myung-bo made the next kick to give the hosts a berth in the semifinals against three-time champions Germany.

The Germans played with patience and discipline against the high-tempo South Koreans. Star midfielder Michael Ballack made the decisive play near the end of the second half. Center forward Oliver Neuville was playing the ball out on the right wing, attacking down the line. Ballack moved up to fill Neuville's spot in the middle. Neuville played his cross low and back toward the middle of the box, placing it perfectly for an onrushing Ballack. Lee made the save on the first shot, but Ballack corralled the rebound and knocked it in with his left foot. The goal stood to eliminate the South Koreans 1–0, but it remains the best-ever showing from an Asian side at any World Cup to date.

As expected, Ronaldo and Brazil were the opponents for Germany in the final. Ronaldo had already scored six goals in the tournament so far. Against the Germans, he added two more 12 minutes apart in the second half to give Brazil a fifth title.

Gianluigi Buffon and Italy suffered a controversial loss to South Korea in 2002, but found redemption by winning the World Cup in 2006

2006 World Cup

Following the strong showing by the Asian countries in 2002, FIFA took a qualifying spot from UEFA and awarded it to Asia, giving the AFC four guaranteed spots. The spot previously given to the defending champion became a playoff spot, so the new breakdown of spot allotment was: three from North America, four from Asia, four from South America, five from Africa, thirteen from Europe, and two playoff spots that went to either Asia, North America, South America, or Oceania. The host nation retained an automatic bid.

In 2006, Buffon and the Italians were on a mission to make up for what they felt was the injustice that was done to them in 2002. Buffon was especially strong, allowing just one goal in the group stage as Italy claimed the top spot.

In the round of 16, Italy played Australia in a close match that ended on a very late penalty given five minutes into added time. The 1–0 clean sheet for Buffon put Italy in the quarterfinals against Ukraine. Buffon was unbeatable again as Luca Toni scored two second-half goals, and Italy won 3–0.

In the semifinals against Germany, Ballack and his teammates joined the list of those unable to solve Buffon. Regulation time expired with the match tied 0–0, but Italy scored twice in the final two minutes of extra time to win 2–0. Another clean sheet win for Buffon put Italy in the final against France.

Early goals by Zidane for France and Marco Materazzi for Italy stood through regulation, and the final went to extra time. In the 110th minute, Zidane and Materazzi were jogging up the field together with the ball downfield in the French end. Materazzi said something to Zidane that angered the French star, who turned and drove the crown of his head into Materazzi's chest. The referee immediately showed the French captain a red card, and he was unavailable not only for the remainder of the match but for the penalty shootout that followed as well. David Trezeguet missed the second kick for France, the only failure in the shootout, so Italy claimed victory and a fourth World Cup title.

French captain Zinedine Zidane's infamous head-butt of Italy's Marco Materazzi from the 2006 final was immortalized in this 2012 sculpture by French artist Adel Abdessemed

TEXT-DEPENDENT QUESTIONS:

1. Which country hosted the 1990 World Cup?

2. Who was the leading goal scorer for France in the 1998 World Cup final match?

3. How many World Cup titles did Italy have after the 2006 World Cup?

RESEARCH PROJECT:

Examine the career of 2006 World Cup champion Gianluigi Buffon, the Italian goalkeeper. Write a brief report detailing his career accomplishments at both the international and club levels.

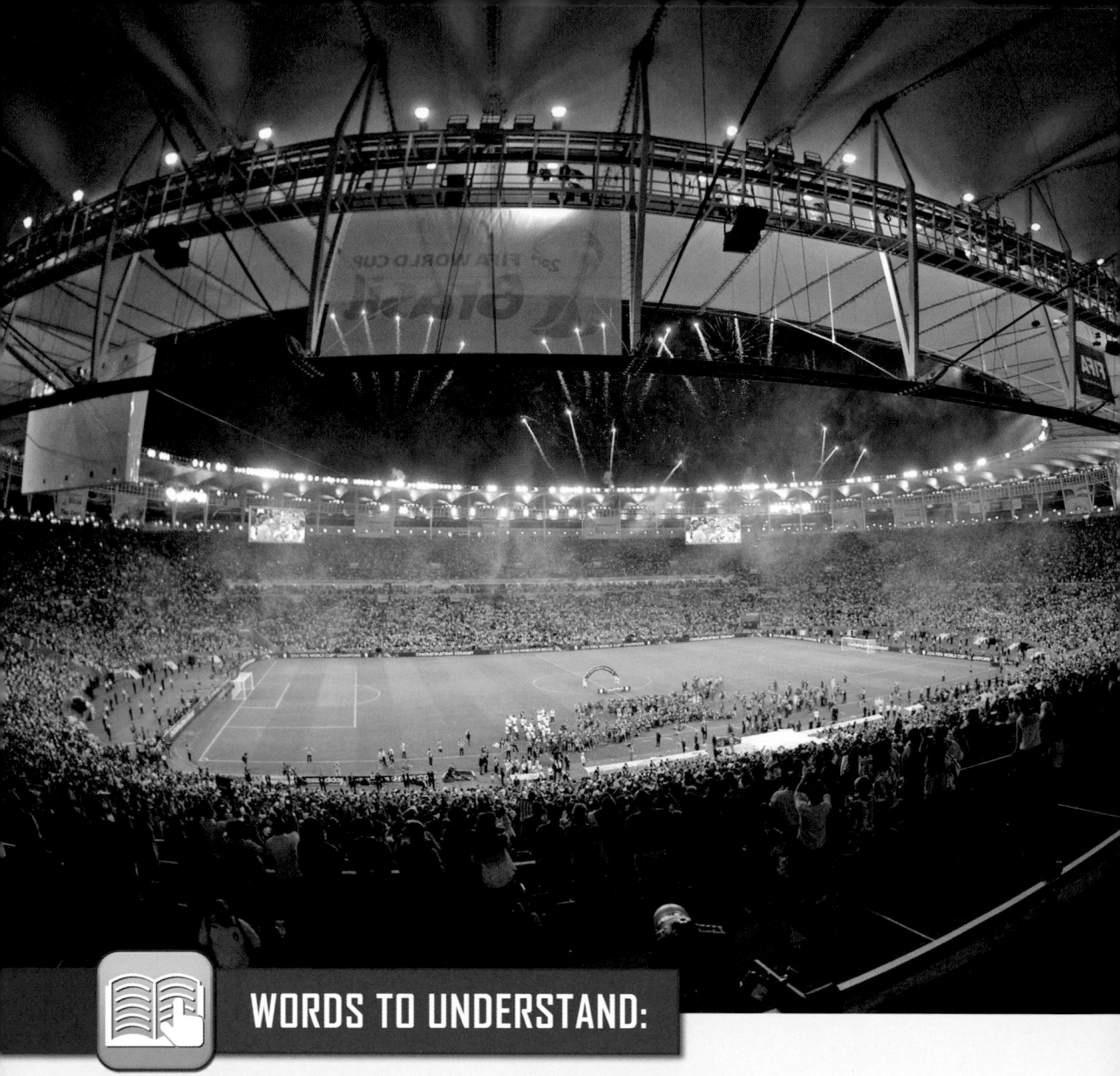

WORDS TO UNDERSTAND:

doping: the use of a substance or technique to illegally improve athletic performance

perennial: regularly repeated or renewed; continuing without interruption

ratified: gave legal approval to (as by a vote)

vertebra: one of the small bones that are linked together to form the backbone

CHAPTER 5

VUVUZELAS TO VOLGOGRAD (2010–18)

In 2001, FIFA **ratified** a policy that hosting duties for the World Cup would rotate between each of its confederations, beginning with Africa. The policy came about due to a bribery scandal around the selection of Germany as the host for the 2006 event. Therefore, only African nations were permitted to bid for the 2010 tournament, and only South American countries were eligible to bid for the 2014 World Cup. In 2004, South Africa won the right to host in 2010. With the bidding for 2014, however, problems arose. Brazil was the only country to submit a formal bid. FIFA did not like the lack of competition for bids that resulted from restricting bidding to one confederation at a time. Therefore in 2007, shortly after Brazil won with an unopposed 2014 bid, the rotational policy was abandoned. Currently, the sole restriction for bids is that they can only come from countries whose confederations have not hosted either of the previous two World Cups.

2010 World Cup

The 2010 World Cup in South Africa may well be best remembered for the vuvuzela. This is the name of the two-foot-long horns that have been popular with fans at football matches in South Africa since the 1980s. For the 2010 World Cup, plastic versions of the unique sounding horns were mass produced and heavily marketed, and their constant buzzing sound could be heard throughout every stadium and by fans watching all over the world.

The 2010 World Cup in South Africa is remembered almost as much for the constant buzz of vuvuzelas as it is for the action on the pitch

On the pitch, the tournament is remembered for the dominance of La Roja, which is the nickname of the

Spanish captain Iker Casillas won the Golden Glove at the 2010 World Cup, giving up just two goals all tournament

team from Spain. Spain came in as one of the heavy favorites to win the tournament along with Brazil. The group stage started badly for the Spaniards, however, as they were upset 1–0 in the opening match against 24th-ranked Switzerland. Striker David Villa got La Roja back on track with a pair of goals against Honduras in the next match, a 2–0 Spain win. Then Villa and Andrés Iniesta each scored to beat Chile 2–1 in the third match to win the group.

In the round of 16, Spain faced Portugal and its ever-dangerous forward Cristiano Ronaldo, one of the best players in the world. The Spanish defense, led by right back Sergio Ramos, never wavered against the Portuguese, and Villa again supplied the offense in a 1–0 win.

The quarterfinals opponent for Spain was a surprising Paraguay side, which came into the tournament ranked 31st in the world. This remains the best World Cup performance in the history of Paraguay, and keeper Justo Villar and his squad fought hard against La Roja. Villar's Spanish counterpart, keeper and captain Iker Casillas, saved a penalty kick in the 56th minute. Not to be outdone, Villar also saved a penalty just a few minutes later. At first it appeared Spain's Xabi Alonso had scored on the kick, but the referee demanded it be retaken due to encroachment against Spain. Villar stopped Alonso on the retry. In the end, Villa's fifth goal of the tournament in the 83rd minute secured the win.

The mighty Germans awaited them in the semifinals and the two sides played a tight defensive match well into the second half. Casillas stood his ground, and when center back Carles Puyol scored in the 73rd minute, it was all Spain needed to advance to the final.

This was the first final match appearance for Spain, and they faced a very hot side from the Netherlands, which had beaten Brazil in the quarterfinals. The match was hard fought and very physical, with 14 yellow card issued throughout regulation and extra time. With the score still 0–0 after 19 minutes of extra time, the physical play caught up to the Dutch. Center back John Heitinga was one of seven Dutch players carrying a yellow card received in the match. With Spain in possession about 30 yards from the Dutch goal, Heitinga was marking Iniesta when Iniesta spun to run by him just as Spain's Xavi chipped the ball over his head. In desperation while giving chase, Heitinga reached out and grabbed Iniesta, spurring the referee to issue him another yellow card, for which he was sent off. It was just seven minutes later, with the team down to 10 men, when Dutch defender Gregory van der Wiel stretched his leg out to prevent a Fernando Torres cross from getting through to Iniesta. Van der Wiel deflected the ball right to Spain's Cesc Fabregas, and worse, fell down while making the play. This left Iniesta unmarked, and Fabregas made the pass to set up Iniesta's World Cup-winning goal.

2014 World Cup

The 2014 World Cup in Brazil featured some great performances from South American superstars playing in front of familiar fans. The most notable were Lionel Messi of Argentina and Neymar of Brazil.

Argentina and Brazil both came in to the competition ranked in the top five in the world, along with Germany, Portugal, and defending champions and top-ranked Spain. Spain and Portugal had disappointing tournaments and were eliminated in the group stage. Argentina, Brazil, and Germany all won their groups to advance. Messi scored four times in Argentina's three group-stage wins. Neymar also had four goals for Brazil in the opening round.

In the round of 16, all three remaining favorites went to extra time in their matches. Brazil had a tough match against Chile, winning via a penalty kick shootout after the match was tied 1–1 following extra time. Argentina needed an extra-time goal to eliminate Switzerland 1–0. Germany won 2–1 versus Algeria, with all three goals coming in extra time.

In the quarterfinals, an early Mats Hummels goal stood up for the 1–0 Germany win over France. The same went for Argentina against Belgium, with Gonzalo Higuaín scoring the only goal of the match. Brazil eliminated Colombia and their scoring sensation James Rodríguez 2–1, but it was a costly victory as Neymar was lost for the tournament when he suffered a fractured **vertebra** with two minutes

Neymar had four goals in the opening round for Brazil in 2014, but his injury in the quarterfinals was a blow his team could not overcome

SIDEBAR: PRINCE OF PARIS

It is impossible to know what might have been had Neymar not been injured in the final minutes of a quarterfinal win over Colombia at the 2014 World Cup. Would the healthy Brazilian superstar have been so impactful that he could have reversed the fortunes of his team in a humiliating 7–1 semifinal loss to eventual champions Germany? No one knows the answer, but it is certainly too easy to say one player cannot make that kind of difference. This player is one that many feel can be extremely impactful indeed.

Paris Saint-Germain CEO Nasser Al-Khelaifi is one of those people. As the top man at the top club in France, he chose to pay more than $260 million to secure Neymar's transfer from Barcelona. Neymar spent four extremely successful seasons riding shotgun for Lionel Messi at Barcelona. He made his debut for PSG in August of 2017, now in the driver's seat as the new prince of Paris.

left in the match. To make matters worse for the hosts, captain Thiago Silva picked up a yellow card in the second half, meaning he would be suspended for the semifinals for getting too many cards.

This set up a semifinal encounter between Brazil and Germany while Argentina took on the Netherlands. Without their two key players, the Brazilians were no match for the Germans, who showed no mercy in embarrassing Brazil in front of their home fans 7–1, including five goals in the first 29 minutes. The other semifinal was much more competitive. Argentina and the Netherlands played 120 minutes without a goal. Following extra time, the teams went to a penalty kick shootout. Argentina keeper Sergio Romero set

A miss by the Netherland's Wesley Sneijder in the penalty kick shootout in the 2014 World Cup semifinals against Argentina led to the elimination of the Dutch

the tone, guessing correctly in diving to his left to stop center back Ron Vlaar, the first Dutch shooter. Messi started it off for Argentina by scoring on the team's first kick. The next two players also made their kicks, making it 2–1 to Argentina and bringing up the excellent Dutch midfielder Wesley Sneijder. On Sneijder's attempt, Romero guessed correctly again, going right this time and getting his left hand on the ball for the save. Argentina did not miss a kick, winning the shootout 4–2.

The final was a close affair, with neither team able to score in regulation despite several chances, mostly by Higuaín for Argentina and substitute André Schürrle for Germany. In extra time, Schürrle's hustle paid off as he sprinted down the left side with the ball and then skillfully split two defenders with his cross. The cross found the chest of another substitute, Mario Götze, who took the ball on his chest at the top-left corner of the six-yard box and volleyed it into the net left-footed before it ever hit the ground. Germany became the third team to capture at least four World Cup titles.

Argentina's Lionel Messi controls the ball against Germany's Mats Hummels in the 2014 World Cup final match. Germany won 1–0

GERMANY			ARGENTINA
MANUEL NEUER	1	1	SERGIO ROMERO
(C) PHILIPP LAHM	16	4	PABLO ZABALETA
JEROME BOATENG	20	15	MARTIN DEMICHELIS
MATS HUMMELS	5	2	EZEQUIEL GARRAY
BENEDIKT HOWEDES	4	16	MARCOS ROJO
CHRISTOPH KRAMER	23	6	LUCAS BIGLIA
BASTIAN SCHWEINSTEIGER	7	14	JAVIER MASCHERANO
THOMAS MULLER	13	8	ENZO PEREZ
TONI KROOS	18	9	GONZALO HIGUAIN
MESUT OZIL	8	22	EZEQUIEL LAVEZZI
MIROSLAV KLOSE	11	10	LIONEL MESSI (C)

00:00

Watch highlights from a back-and-forth affair between Germany and Argentina for the 2014 World Cup trophy

2018 World Cup

Perennial favorite Brazil was the first to qualify a side for the 2018 World Cup in Russia, clinching a spot on March 28, 2017. Brazil was followed closely by Iran and Japan from Asia, Mexico from North America, and Belgium, the first of 13 teams to qualify out of Europe.

Also qualifying, of course, is host nation Russia. Matches will be held at sites from Sochi and Volgograd in the south to Saint Petersburg and Kaliningrad further north. Despite the enormity of the country, all tournament sites are concentrated in or close to European Russia, which is relatively compact by comparison. This will reduce travel times for the players.

Kaliningrad Stadium, seen here under construction in June of 2017, is one of the sites for the 2018 World Cup in Russia

The selection of Russia as host was not without controversy. In 2015, the United States Federal Bureau of Investigation (FBI) announced it would be investigating the bid selection process surrounding the awards to Russia in 2018 and Qatar in 2022. There have been allegations of widespread corruption (including $150 million in bribes) at the time the votes were cast in 2010.

Disgraced ex-president of FIFA Sepp Blatter was ousted and banned for six years by the FIFA ethics committee in early 2016. In an interview with Russia's Tass news agency in 2015, Blatter admitted that Russia was the agreed-upon choice for the 2018 host before any voting was done. The FA threatened to have England boycott that event, as the English were furious at having spent more than $20 million to bid on a fixed outcome. Many in the soccer world called for Russia to be removed as host.

Under a cloud of corruption allegations, FIFA president Sepp Blatter was banned from the sport for six years in 2016

Then in June of 2017, allegations of **doping** by Russian athletes, including the 2014 national soccer team, surfaced. The World Anti-Doping Agency (WADA) has accused Russia of being state sponsors of doping and of protecting athletes who are drug cheats. This led to further calls for Russia to be removed as host. Despite all this controversy, it appears the world will nonetheless go to Russia for the World Cup in 2018.

Despite these persistent clouds, there is plenty to look forward to in 2018. The usual cast of countries will again be favored, but many are led by exciting new players looking to make their name on the sport's biggest stage.

Brazil qualified easily for the 2018 World Cup, but then they always do, having never missed a tournament. With Neymar leading the way, Brazil will be dangerous as usual. Neymar's supporting cast includes Philippe Coutinho, Willian, and 21-year-old sensation Gabriel Jesus.

Germany will be heard from in 2018 because they always are. A constant at the top of the FIFA rankings, the Germans have made it to at least the quarterfinals of every World Cup since 1982. The defending champions boast a roster likely to include the world's top keeper in Manuel Neuer, along with superstars Toni Kroos, Mats Hummels, and Thomas Müller. New blood comes in the form of Julian Draxler and Joshua Kimmich.

Will Argentine Lionel Messi be able to clear that last hurdle and claim a World Cup title? It is the only thing in soccer he has not yet accomplished, coming so close in losing the final to the Germans in 2014. Arguably the world's best player, Messi will be joined in 2018 by veterans Sergio Agüero and Ángel Di María, who will ride shotgun as usual.

Portugal's captain Cristiano Ronaldo will have plenty of support from youthful teammates as he tries to win his country's first World Cup in 2018

The other man in the best player argument is Portugal's Cristiano Ronaldo, who is also looking for a path to soccer's mountaintop. Ronaldo made the semifinals with Portugal in 2006, and the 2018 team may be good enough to get the 33-year-old veteran there again. Young stars-in-the-making Raphaël Guerreiro and Bernardo Silva will entertain along the way.

France has the advantage of having youthful veterans. Paul Pogba reached 50 caps before his 25th birthday in 2018, and Antoine Griezmann was just one year older when he hit that milestone. The French have even more impressive young players as well, including 25-year-old center back Raphaël Varane and 19-year-old striker Kylian Mbappé.

In the end, it will all come down to the game on the pitch and the players who make it look so effortless.

TEXT-DEPENDENT QUESTIONS:

1. In what year was South Africa awarded the 2010 World Cup?

2. Which two key players did Brazil lose before the semifinal against Germany at the 2014 World Cup?

3. Name two players for France to reach 50 caps before turning 26 years old.

RESEARCH PROJECT:

Pick three young up-and-coming stars on the international soccer scene and write a brief profile of each, detailing how they got started in the game, their accomplishments to date, and why you think they may be the next big thing in soccer.

Advantage: when a player is fouled but play is allowed to continue because the team that suffered the foul is in a better position than they would have been had the referee stopped the game.

Armband: removable colored band worn around the upper arm by a team's captain, to signify that role.

Bend: skill attribute in which players strike the ball in a manner that applies spin, resulting in the flight of the ball curving, or bending, in mid-air.

Bicycle kick: a specific scoring attempt made by a player with their back to the goal. The player throws their body into the air, makes a shearing movement with the legs to get one leg in front of the other, and attempts to play the ball backwards over their own head, all before returning to the ground. Also known as an *overhead kick.*

Box: common name for the penalty area, a rectangular area measuring 44 yards (40.2 meters) by 18 yards (16.5 meters) in front of each goal. Fouls occurring within this area result in a penalty kick.

Club: collective name for a team, and the organization that runs it.

CONCACAF: acronym for the *Confederation of North, Central American and Caribbean Association Football,* the governing body of the sport in North and Central America and the Caribbean; pronounced "kon-ka-kaff."

CONMEBOL: acronym for the South American Football Association, the governing body of the sport in South America; pronounced "kon-me-bol."

Corner kick: kick taken from within a 1-yard radius of the corner flag; a method of restarting play when a player plays the ball over their own goal line without a goal being scored.

Cross: delivery of the ball into the penalty area by the attacking team, usually from the area between the penalty box and the touchline.

Dead ball: situation when the game is restarted with the ball stationary; i.e., a free kick.

Defender: one of the four main positions in soccer. Defenders are positioned in front of the goalkeeper and have the principal role of keeping the opposition away from their goal.

Dribbling: when a player runs with the ball at their feet under close control.

Flag: small rectangular flag attached to a handle, used by an assistant referee to signal that they have seen a foul or other infraction take place. "The flag is up" is a common expression for when the assistant referee has signaled for an offside.

Flick-on: when a player receives a pass from a teammate and, instead of controlling it, touches the ball with their head or foot while it is moving past them, with the intent of helping the ball reach another teammate.

Forward: one of the four main positions in football. Strikers are the players closest to the opposition goal, with the principal role of scoring goals. Also known as a *striker* or *attacker*.

Free kick: the result of a foul outside the penalty area given against the offending team. Free kicks can be either direct (shot straight toward the goal) or indirect (the ball must touch another player before a goal can be scored).

Fullback: position on either side of the defense, whose job is to try to prevent the opposing team attacking down the wings.

Full-time: the end of the game, signaled by the referees whistle. Also known as the *final whistle*.

Goal difference: net difference between goals scored and goals conceded. Used to differentiate league or group stage positions when clubs are tied on points.

Goalkeeper: one of the four main positions in soccer. This is the player closest to the goal a team is defending. They are the only player on the pitch that can handle the ball in open play, although they can only do so in the penalty area.

Goal kick: method of restarting play when the ball is played over the goal line by a player of the attacking team without a goal being scored.

Goal-line technology: video replay or sensor technology systems used to determine whether the ball has crossed the line for a goal or not.

Hat trick: when a player scores three goals in a single match.

Header: using the head as a means of playing or controlling the ball.

Linesman: another term for the assistant referee that patrols the sideline with a flag monitoring play for fouls, offsides, and out of bounds.

Long ball: attempt to distribute the ball a long distance down the field without the intention to pass it to the feet of the receiving player.

Manager: the individual in charge of the day-to-day running of the team. Duties of the manager usually include overseeing training sessions, designing tactical plays, choosing the team's formation, picking the starting eleven, and making tactical switches and substitutions during games.

Man of the Match: an award, often decided by pundits or sponsors, given to the best player in a game.

Midfielder: one of the four main positions in soccer. Midfielders are positioned between the defenders and forwards.

OFC: initials for the *Oceania Football Confederation*, the governing body of the sport in Oceania.

Offside: a player is offside if they are in their opponent's half of the field and closer to the goal line than both the second-last defender and the ball at the moment the ball is played to them by a teammate. Play is stopped and a free kick is given against the offending team.

Offside trap: defensive tactical maneuver, in which each member of a team's defense will simultaneously step forward as the ball is played forward to an opponent, in an attempt to put that opponent in an offside position.

Own goal: where a player scores a goal against their own team, usually as the result of an error.

Penalty area: rectangular area measuring 44 yards (40.2 meters) by 18 yards (16.5 meters) in front of each goal; commonly called *the box*.

Penalty kick: kick taken 12 yards (11 meters) from goal, awarded when a team commits a foul inside its own penalty area.

Penalty shootout: method of deciding a match in a knockout competition, which has ended in a draw after full-time and extra-time. Players from each side take turns to attempt to score a penalty kick against the opposition goalkeeper. Sudden death is introduced if scores are level after each side has taken five penalties.

Red card: awarded to a player for either a single serious cautionable offence or following two yellow cards. The player receiving the red card is compelled to leave the game for the rest of its duration, and that player's team is not allowed to replace him with another player. A player receiving the red card is said to have been *sent off* or *ejected*.

Side: another word for team.

Stoppage time: an additional number of minutes at the end of each half, determined by the match officials, to compensate for time lost during the game. Informally known by various names, including *injury time* and *added time*.

Striker: see Forward.

Studs: small points on the underside of a player's boots to help prevent slipping. A tackle in which a player directs their studs toward an opponent is referred to as a *studs-up challenge*, and is a foul punishable by a red card.

Substitute: a player who is brought on to the pitch during a match in exchange for a player currently in the game.

Sweeper: defender whose role is to protect the space between the goalkeeper and the rest of the defense.

Tackle: method of a player winning the ball back from an opponent, achieved either by using the feet to take possession from the opponent, or making a slide tackle to knock the ball away. A tackle in which the opposing player is kicked before the ball is punishable by either a free kick or penalty kick. Dangerous tackles may also result in a yellow or red card.

Throw-in: method of restarting play. Involves a player throwing the ball from behind a touch line after an opponent has kicked it out.

Trap: skill performed by a player, whereupon the player uses their foot (or, less commonly, their chest or thigh) to bring an airborne or falling ball under control.

UEFA: acronym for *Union of European Football Associations*, the governing body of the sport in Europe; pronounced "you-eh-fa."

Winger: wide midfield player whose primary focus is to provide crosses into the penalty area. Alternatively known as a *wide midfielder*.

World Cup: commonly refers to the men's FIFA World Cup tournament held every four years, but is also associated with the FIFA Women's World Cup, international tournaments for youth football (such as the FIFA U-20 World Cup), and the FIFA Club World Cup.

Yellow card: shown by the referee to a player who commits a cautionable offence. If a player commits two cautionable offences in a match, they are shown a second yellow card, followed by a red card, and are then sent off. Also known as a *caution* or a *booking*.

FURTHER READING, INTERNET RESOURCES & VIDEO CREDITS:

Further Reading:

Bailey, Diane. *Great Moments in World Cup History* (World Soccer Books). New York, NY: Rosen Publishing, 2010.

Colley, Rupert. *The World Cup: A History*. London, UK: Rupertcolley.com, 2014.

Markovits, Andrei. *Offside: Soccer and American Exceptionalism*. Princeton, NJ: Princeton University Press, 2014.

Internet Resources:

FIFA: www.fifa.com

History of the World Cup: www.historyoftheworldcup.com

Goal: www.goal.com

Video Credits:

Chapter 1:
Cristiano Check out this short recap of the 1938 World Cup final:
http://x-qr.net/1Fv9

Chapter 2:
Watch the highlights of the England-West Germany final from the 1966 World Cup:
http://x-qr.net/1FGc

Chapter 3:
An extraordinary display of skill and teamwork leads to a perfect Brazilian goal at the 1970 World Cup:
http://x-qr.net/1FQj

Chapter 4:
Check out the highlights of the 1994 World Cup final between Italy and Brazil:
http://x-qr.net/1Dda

Chapter 5:
Watch highlights from a back-and-forth affair between Germany and Argentina for the 2014 World Cup trophy:
http://x-qr.net/1HM1

INDEX

Andrew Luke

ABOUT THE AUTHOR:

Andrew Luke is a former journalist, reporting on both sports and general news for many years at television stations in various locations across the US affiliated with NBC, CBS and Fox. Prior to his journalism career he worked with the Boston Red Sox Major League baseball team. An avid writer and sports enthusiast, he has authored 26 other books on sports topics. In his downtime Andrew enjoys family time with his wife and two young children and attending hockey and baseball games in his home city of Pittsburgh, PA.

PICTURE CREDITS: